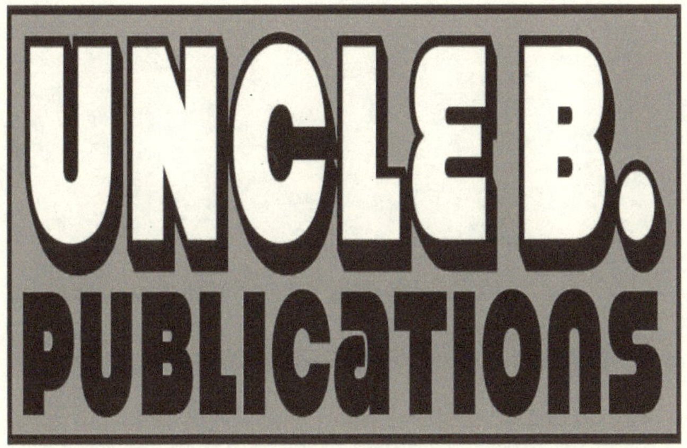

INDIANAPOLIS

Whiskey Stories

BY JIM TOWNS

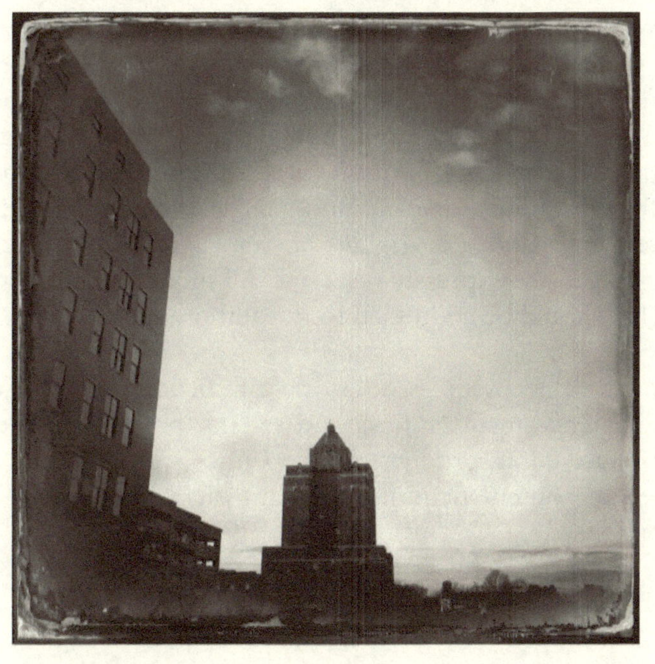

WITH PHOTOGRAHS BY THE AUTHOR

WHISKEY STORIES

First Printing, March 2022

ISBN: 978-1-957034-05-8

TABLE OF CONTENTS

WHISKEY STORIES

FOREWORD

I didn't set out to write a book of poetry. This is something that happened along the way. Thank you for reading.

About the words:

Every story I write originally comes from a vague idea. Some of these ideas are strong enough to evolve into a completed screenplay. Others have potential to be novellas, or short stories. But many are still gestating, waiting maybe for a spark to let them evolve to the next stage. Some, frankly, exist really as just a vibe, and many of those are what follow. Many of these little snapshots of a story may never get past this stage, and I'm really okay with that.

The ideas contained herein are sometimes dark, sometimes hopeful. Sometimes they are humorous in an inappropriate manner, and I apologize on their behalf for their lack of class. Hopefully, above all else, they are impactful and ring true. That, after all, is the goal.

I have no delusions that I'm any kind of a sonneteer. Mostly I just try to listen to what the words and phrases want, and break them into something that forces the reader to slow down and savor the depth of the sounds in their mind. Reading is a wholly unique kind of silent auditory discipline, and it's too easy to forget that.

About the pictures:

The images accompanying these pieces represent twenty years of photography, from Polaroid to 35mm film to DSLR to mobile phone camera. They were taken in Pennsylvania, Massachusetts, California, France, Japan, the Caribbean and elsewhere. Wherever I am, I enjoy photographing small things and big things: showcasing a miniature world that exists within a macrocosm, infinite in its scale.

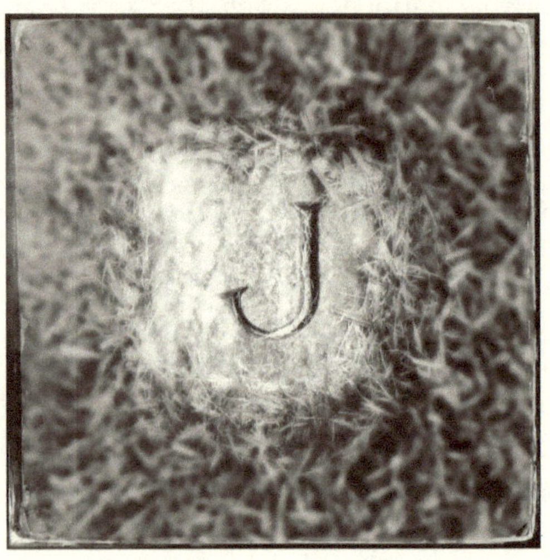

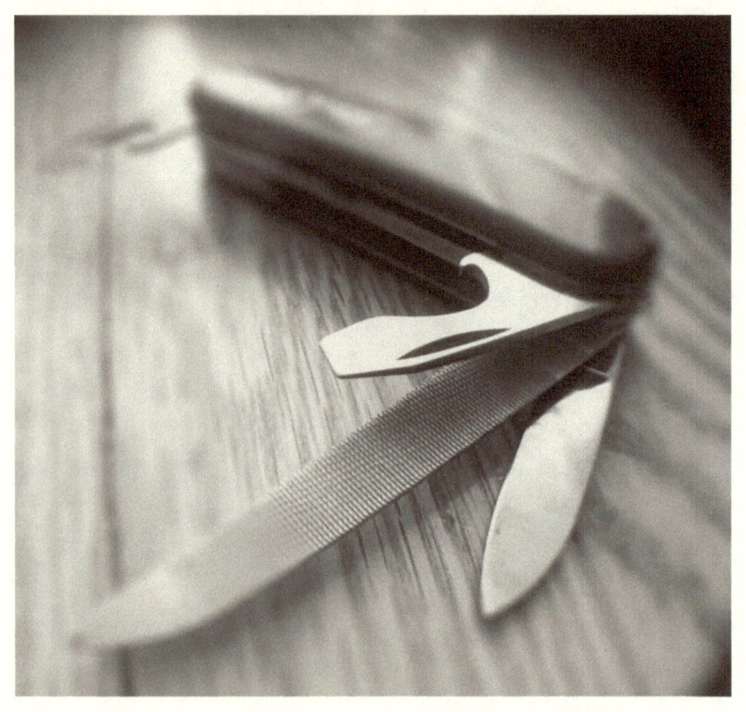

BROKEN BLADE

I inherited a hand-me-down Swiss Army Knife:

Can Opener/Corkscrew/Screwdriver

Nail file/Scissors/Toothpick

Small Blade....

The Big Blade is snapped.

Broken off right at the base.

How did it happen?

Prying open a can?

Cutting at some wood?

Gutting a fish?

(the knife has better tools for all these things)

After all, the Big Blade is the centerpiece of the knife: its primary tool.

Everything else is just a bonus, really. Right?

Why it's called a Swiss Army KNIFE.

When the Thing that defines the Thing is missing, is the Thing still the Thing?

Now there's this empty void in the pocket of the tool.

A hollow slit.

Still useful, but...

Is the thing now incapable of fulfilling its main purpose?

Or do we just make do with the little one?

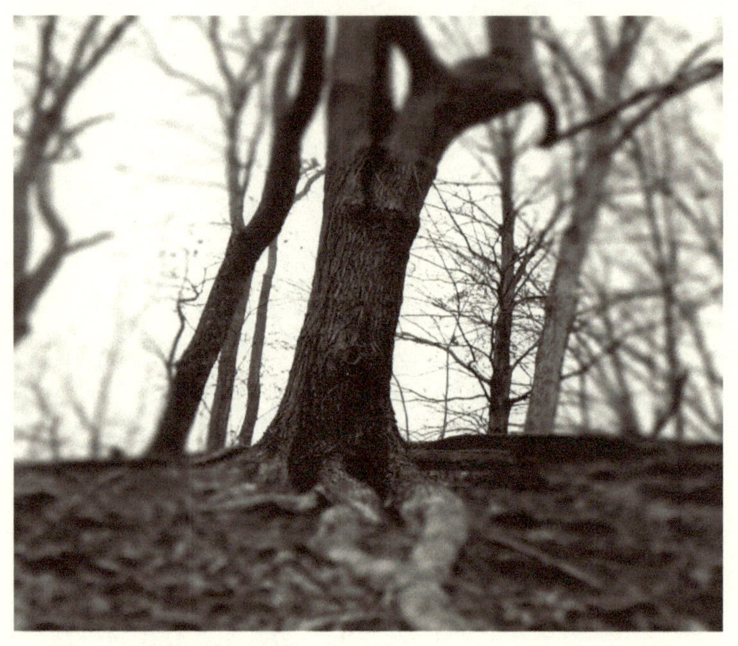

A SHALLOW CREEK

Nothing good

Ever happened

In a shallow creek.

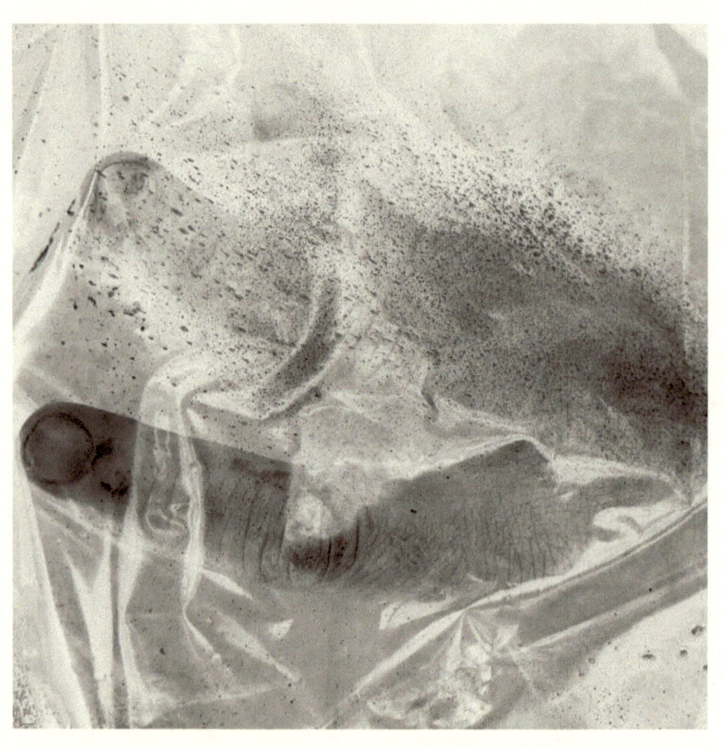

WRAPPED IN PLASTIC

She didn't remember ordering a dead body.

Yet here it was, delivered to her doorstep in a big square cardboard box.

Inside layers of poppy bubble wrap,

And inside that

A dozen sealable plastic bags

(the good quality, brand name ones)

of various sizes.

Inside each of those,

A body part:

a foot,

a forearm,

a bit of torso.

Ears, nose.

Genitals.

And one single photo

Taped to the inside of the lid,
Showing what he'd looked like
assembled.
She remembered him.
She remembered the yelling, the cursing
The blows, the threats, the tears.
Years ago in another city when she'd had a different
name.
There was no sender's address listed.
It was difficult to know what to do.
She'd spent years worried he'd show up again.
And now
here we was.
She lit some candles and opened a bottle
of Pinot Noir.
And had one last dinner with him.
Over the next week,
She threw away the parts

one by one.

Wrapped up in a plastic bag with used kitty litter,

Or inside the Styrofoam shell from takeaway sushi.

Always with food garbage, always in the black trashcan.

Because after all,

you can't recycle shit.

Bit by bit, she threw him away, until there was nothing left.

But an empty

cardboard box.

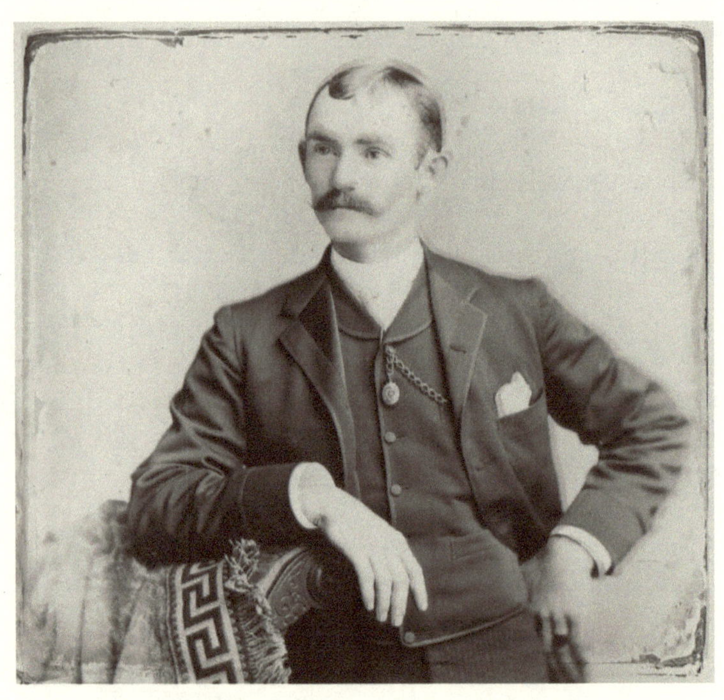

10 Jim Towns

THE GHOSTS OF TEN THOUSAND SNEEZES

I asked the Old Man what was wrong. He said:

"I worry about the ten thousand sneezes, which never came out-

a lifetime's worth, all of them backed up into my head.

Like a legion of ghosts... biding their time,

slowly building pressure, decade after decade after decade after decade..."

As he spoke those words to me, the Old Man's voice slowly trailed off

and he looked away in a distracted sort of fashion.

And just then, his head exploded.

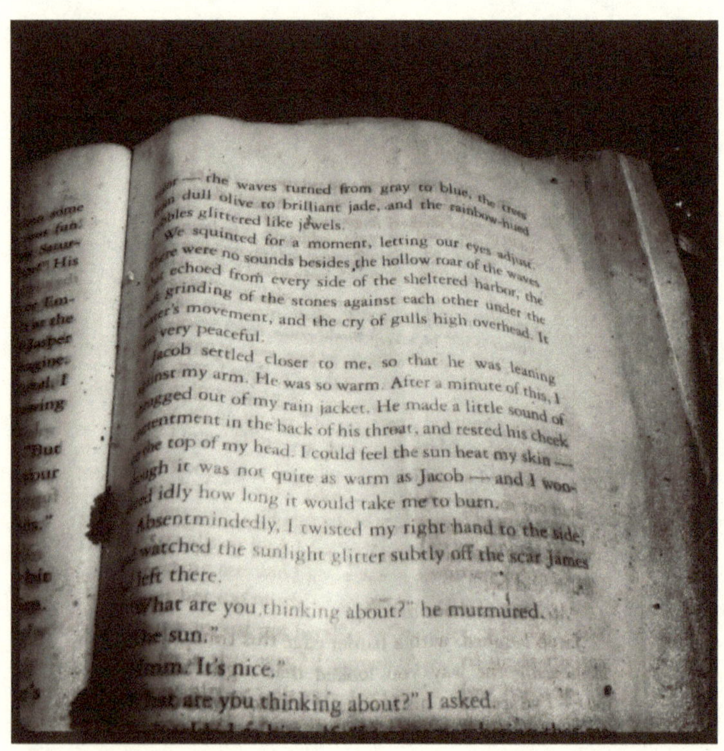
—the waves turned from gray to blue, the trees
dull olive to brilliant jade, and the rainbow-hued
bles glittered like jewels.
We squinted for a moment, letting our eyes adjust.
re were no sounds besides the hollow roar of the waves
echoed from every side of the sheltered harbor, the
grinding of the stones against each other under the
er's movement, and the cry of gulls high overhead. It
very peaceful.
Jacob settled closer to me, so that he was leaning
nst my arm. He was so warm. After a minute of this, I
gged out of my rain jacket. He made a little sound of
entment in the back of his throat, and rested his cheek
he top of my head. I could feel the sun heat my skin —
gh it was not quite as warm as Jacob — and I won-
d idly how long it would take me to burn.
Absentmindedly, I twisted my right hand to the side,
watched the sunlight glitter subtly off the scar James
left there.
What are you thinking about?" he murmured.
he sun."
mm. It's nice."
hat are you thinking about?" I asked.

OVERDUE BOOKS

These things have value, after all.

What were you thinking?

You think you can borrow the collected writings of

Balzac?

Or a book of cat poems,

or The Complete *New Gods* series by Jack Kirby.

And not return them on time?

Your penalty

will be severe.

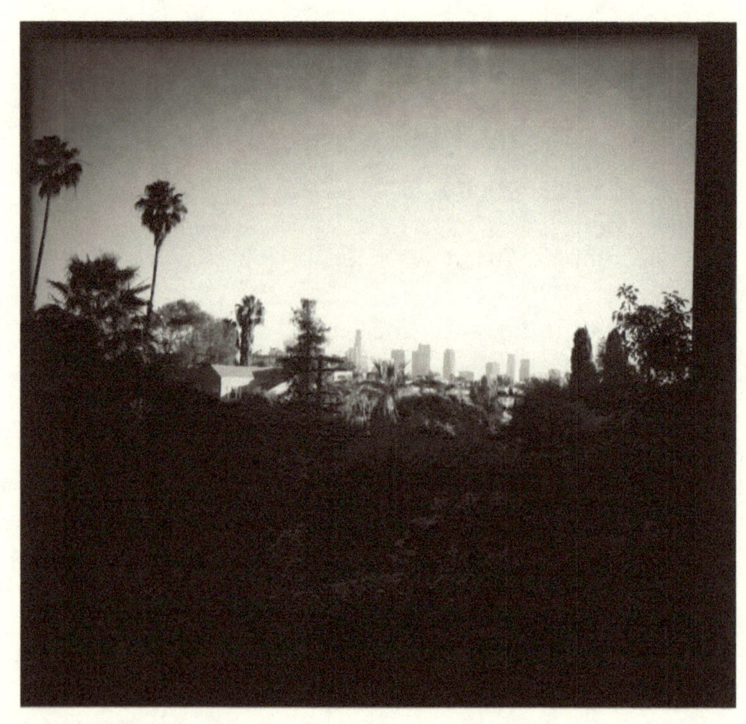

THE TAR PIT

The Plan had been in his head for a decade.
Ever since the school trip to Tar Pits museum;
with its tackily-painted plastic animals
locked in their death throes,
howling at an uncaring sky.
His friend Steve Orlansky had shoved him into a small pool
of oozing black muck.
He'd had to spend the rest of the day with a plastic
sandwich bag tied around his shoe
to keep from sticking to everything.
That day was burned into his memory,
and wasn't going anywhere.

The Plan wasn't an easily accomplishable one.
Many things had to be in place,

and this had taken him years to coordinate:

1). Purchase a house with a basement (rare in Los Angeles).

2). Drill down deep (hard to do quietly, without the neighbors noticing).

3). Maintain the outward appearance of being normal, even boring, to coworkers.

This outward disguise required constant effort, and he found it exhausting at times.

But it was critical, he'd convinced himself.

To his Plan.

Soon it was done.

A bubbling pool of stinking asphalt and bitumen, covering his basement floor.

Waist deep.

Deep enough to be trapped in.

Deep enough to vanish in forever.

Now,

only one more thing to do:

4.) Invite Steve Orlansky over.

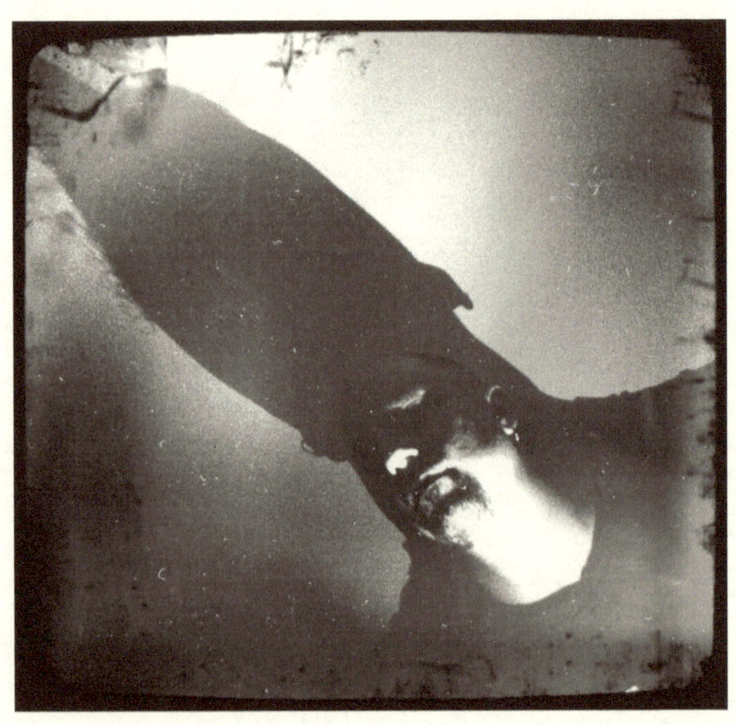

SOUTHBOUND ROY

There was no way back.

Years had passed,

and in those passing years,

Something critical had been lost.

Forever.

Roy knew

he could stand on top of a mountain,

the very top,

and the judging sky would still

loom over him.

Life had crashed over and through him

And most of his bones were now hollow.

Even the ones that weren't,

were now filled with salt.

He was lighter than air,

But held to earth by the ballast

of guilt and loss and failures.

He held faith in no Gods,

But he feared their wrath all just the same.

He knew soon, the time would come,

And he would have to be ready.

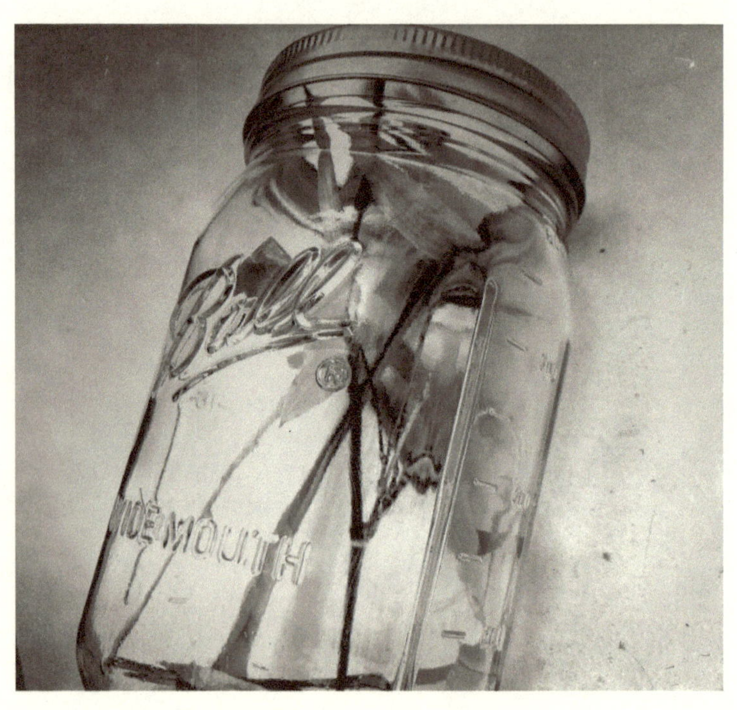
Ball

TWO MIDNIGHTS IN A JAR

It was just a little old mason jar—the kind with the screw-on cap and 'Ball' in raised letters on the side of the glass.

The jar was left over from when my old buddy Troy came by one time to share some of the fine homemade sour mash he cooked up in the hills behind his house. I'd never quite got around to finishing the last of the stuff off, so I'd wager the Midnights have, by now, probably taken on a decided liquor-y flavor, if one were to unscrew the lid and open the jar (which would be a most calamitously bad decision, without doubt).

I'd caught the Midnights in a field down near Eighty-Four, PA, on a summer's evening back in '06. That night was a warm one, and the fireflies were doing their little flickering air ballet all over the tall grass and skunk cabbage. The Midnights were busy watching the fireflies and I just kinda snuck up on them.

I poked a couple holes in the metal cap of the jar so the Midnights could breathe, and threw in a few twigs and things for them to eat and crawl on and stuff. The Midnights seemed contented enough, and just flitted around here and there. They seemed to especially like crawling around on the inside of the glass, so I could get a good view of their dark blue bellies, each filled with what must have been a thousand tiny white specks. They seemed content to bide their time in there—just waiting around for the moment the big hand and the little hand both reached twelve, I guess.

Now I had every intention of letting them loose before that, but around 9:30 I got a phone call from my buddy Troy (who'd given me the jar). Seems he'd had a bad run-in with a combine machine, and had had one of his testicles plucked clean off by the thing. So obviously that ended up taking up most of my attention that particular night, driving him to the hospital to see if they could re-attach his gonad and such.

So I forgot about the Midnights. And before I knew it 11:59 had gone straight on to 12:01, and we'd all missed it, because Midnight was stuck in a crummy little jar.

I was in a bit of a dilemma, then, the next evening. After a good deal of thought and a few beers, I felt like it'd be a bad idea to open the jar and let both the Midnights out, since only one still had a job to do. Of course I couldn't tell which one was tonight's midnight, and which one was last night's (they both looked pretty-much the same to my eye), so I figured the best thing to do was keep them both sealed up. Otherwise we'd have a Midnight flying all around with nothing to do, having missed his big moment the night before. There was just no telling the kind of trouble he'd get into. Best to play it safe, I figured.

So we missed midnight the next night, too. I sat in my room and watched carefully as the big hand on the wall clock swept straight past the twelve to come to rest on the first tick after: 12:01. The whole world lost two minutes over those two nights, and no one seemed to really notice. But I still feel bad about it, all the same.

That's about all that's worth telling. The doctors weren't able to sew poor old Troy's right nut back on, but he's doing fine anyway since he's still got the one.

These days the jar just sits on my mantel. Every couple days I push a few bits of fresh green grass through the little holes in the lid so the Midnights can have a snack. Sometimes they still crawl on the glass and let me stare at their night sky bellies. They seem content enough— like two old timers in a retirement house who've outlived their time, and are resigned to just taking it easy for the duration... until they're called home.

Or maybe it's just the little bit of liquor still in there.

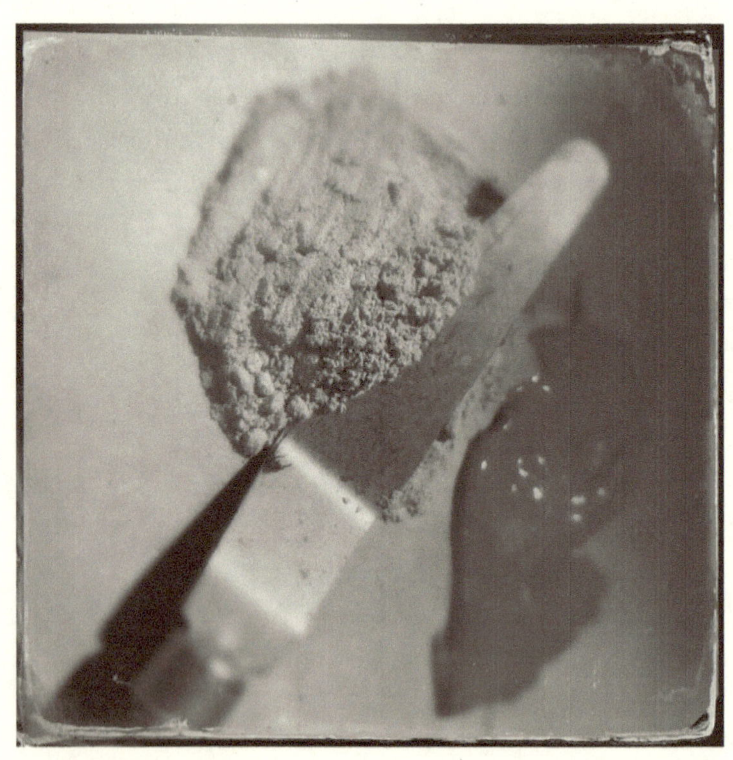

MUMMY BROWN

Many masterpieces

were painted using Mummy Brown.

They'd dig up the remains

Of Egyptian Dead,

Burn them,

And grind the remains into pigment.

Mix with myrrh and white pitch,

And sell to the artists.

Hunt.

Millais.

Rossetti.

Collinson.

And Burne-Jones,

who buried his tube in his backyard

when he learned how

it had come to be.

Ten thousand canvases

Smeared with the remains

Of our ancestors.

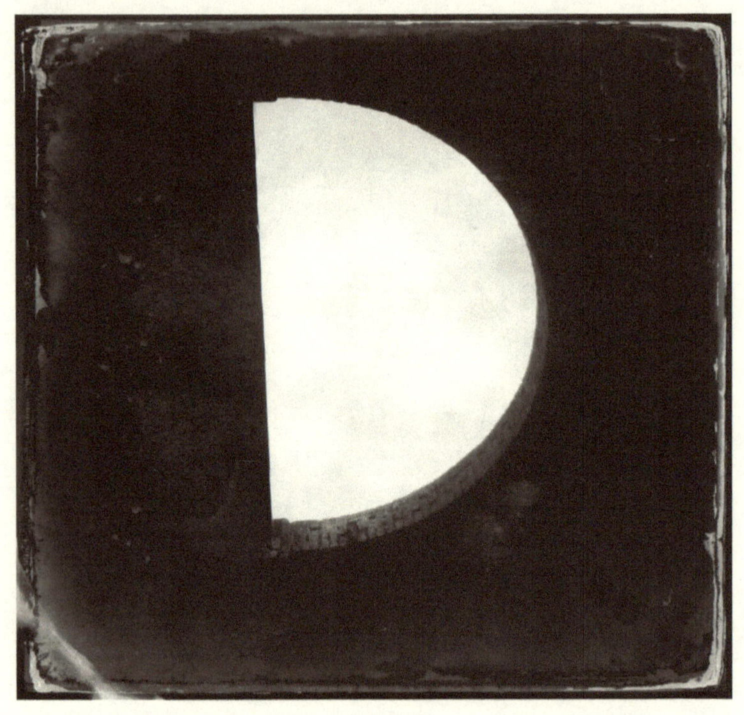

SHOOT THE MOON

It had it coming, that moon.

Other planets have cool sounding moons:

Titan.

Io.

Ganymede.

Phobos and Deimos.

Nix.

But our moon is just called "Moon".

It's stupid. It's like naming a dog "Dog".

Putting the poor, cratered cold sphere out of its misery

Was the only kind thing to do.

So I took up my dad's old shotgun,

Raised it up high into the nighttime sky.

And pulled the trigger.

Boom, Moon.

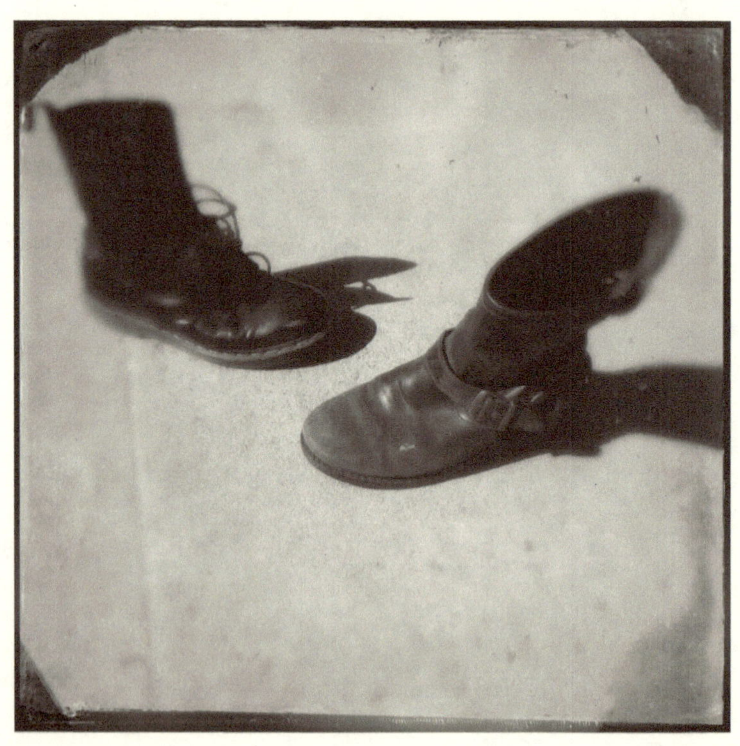

ONE BLACK SHOE AND ONE BROWN SHOE

(for Charles Bukowski)

One summer afternoon I walked down to the bank
after drinking some fine agave tequila.
As I stood in line I looked down and realized
I had left the house wearing one black shoe and one
brown shoe.
Embarrassed, I left the bank, and I haven't had the nerve
to go back since.
I miss my money.

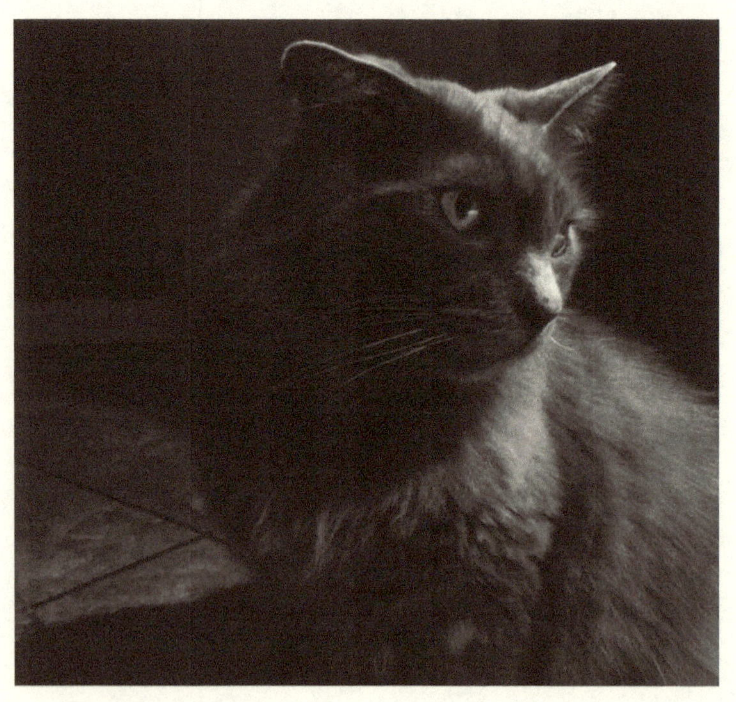

CATS AND GHOSTS

I noticed my cat staring at the ceiling. Really staring.

"Are you staring at a ghost?" I asked him. I thought that was funny.

"Yes," was his reply, still staring.

(this surprised me)

I asked him: "Whose ghost are you staring at?"

He turned to look at me:

"Yours."

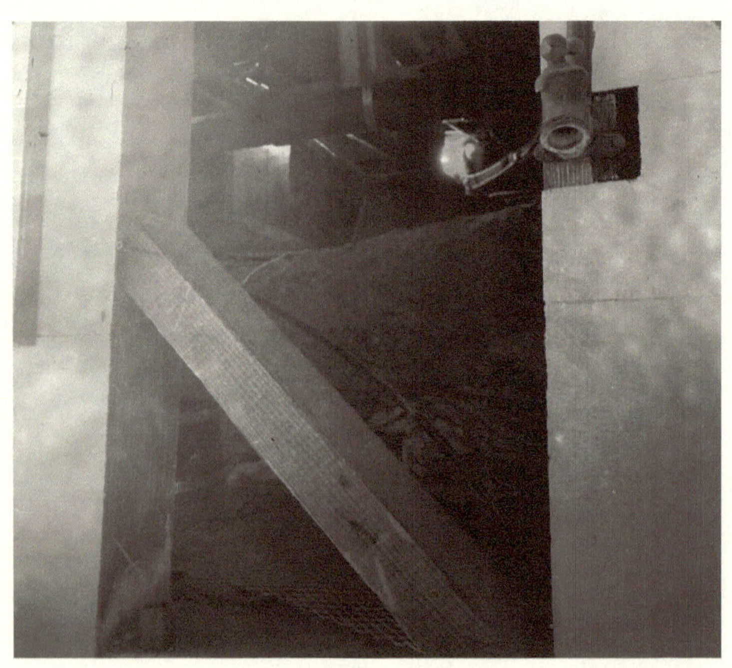

SOMETHING DIED IN THE WALLS

The reek of it had all-but driven him from the house.

A cloying smell of sweet rot that clung to objects:

His clothes.

His hair.

It filled the inside of his nostrils and would not leave.

It had started May 1st.

He had no choice; he finally took a six-pound sledge

And opened up the wall.

He searched with a flash.

He searched with his nose,

but the smell was everywhere he looked.

Rank.

Rotting.

Dead.

He gave up. He decided to take a bath, to get it off him.

But it was still there.

All over him. And he realized

It wasn't coming from inside the walls.

It was coming from inside him.

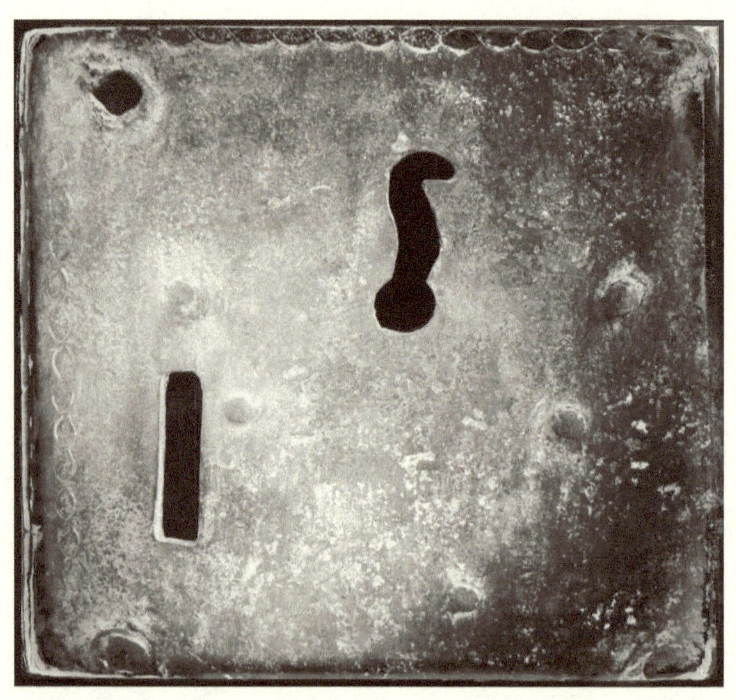

THE LITTLE TOYBOX FILLED WITH HELL

That toy box caused lot of trouble,

for such a little thing.

It's very name

A lie.

No dolls inside,

No toy soldiers.

no balls, games, puzzles

or skates.

Just an empty rectangle

Containing the darkest evil,

I or anyone else had ever seen.

21" x 40"

Depth unknown.

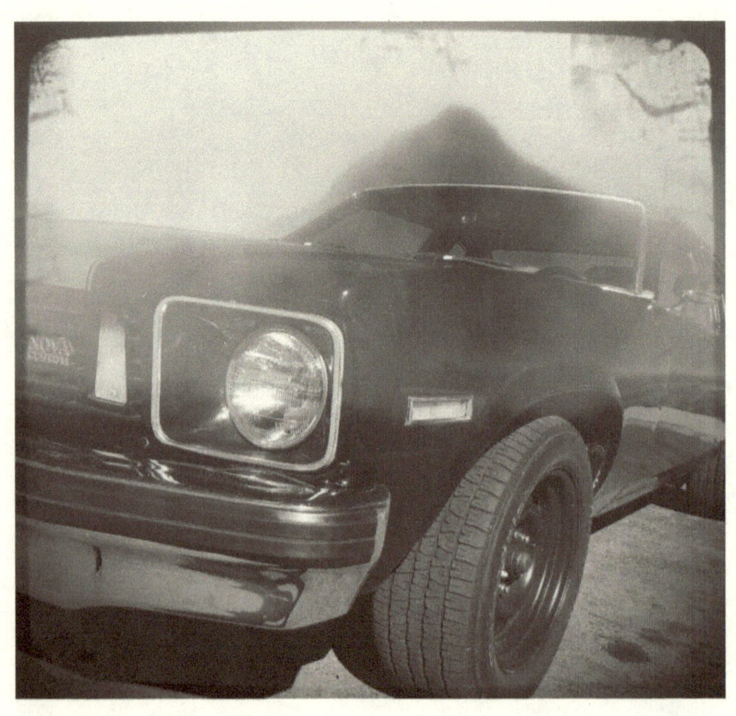

RAMMING SPEED

The girl drove

The car was a bullet fired from a midnight barrel.

Driving, roaring tearing up mile markers and exit signs

Never slowing, never stopping.

A titan engine of speed and death hurtling forward

With bastard abandon and arrogance, eating up the

pavement.

The girl drove

Clothed in a bloodied suit

It once belonged to her would-be killer.

As did the four-wheeled speed machine.

The road burned away to cinders behind her

The girl drove

Her bare foot pressed down on the gas

This was not her first time.

An orgy of blood and mayhem trailed behind her

In her slipstream.

Following her.

Haunting her.

The twin headlights of the car were a bullet wound

stigmata.

The girl drove on

Even though she knew

More enemies lay before her.

Waiting for her.

The girl drove.

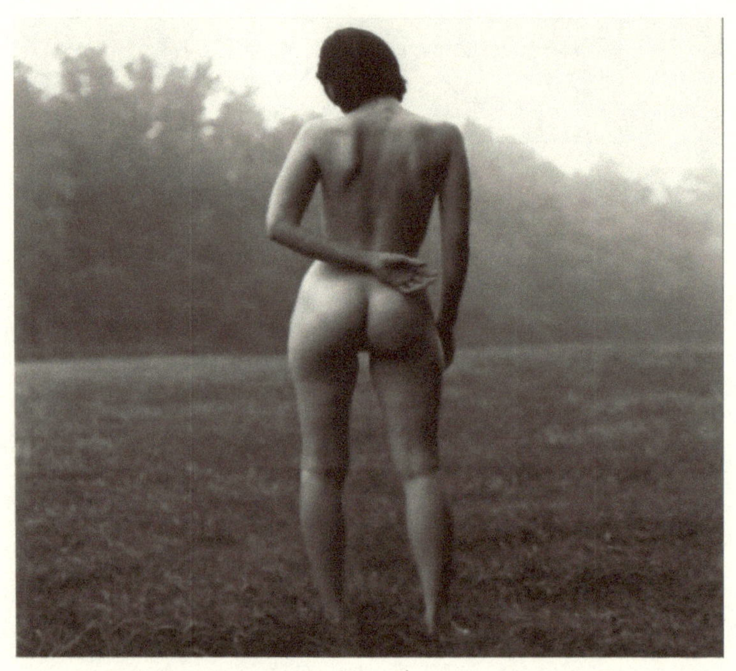

ALL YOU NEED IS A GUN AND A GIRL

(with apologies to Jean-Luc Godard)

I.

Bare, scraggly trees clung tightly to the snow-frosted hills on either side of the ravine.

The girl who walked along the railroad tracks at the bottom was tall and beautiful in mirrored sunglasses, a long coat of no particular color, and tall boots. An old surplus army bag swung on a leather strap from her shoulder. Her long hair hung straight, and occasionally blew about in the chill breeze. Her breath crystalized in the air as she made her way down the rails.

A road.

The girl clambered her way up the snowy slope to highway burn, pausing to catch her breath, giving out big puffs of frost. She looked up the road both ways, and put her thumb out. She stood for a few minutes waiting for a car to pass by. One or two did, but they don't stop.

She dropped the bag on the ground, unbuttoned the front of her coat. The heavy garment slid off her shoulders to hang on the crook of her arms, and revealed she was wearing nothing underneath. Once more she put out her thumb.

The chill breeze stirred her lank hair. Goosebumps stood out all over her bare body. She shivered for a bit, standing like that, until a small yellow car came to an abrupt stop just past her. She pulled up her coat, and picked up her bag.

The window rolled down and the girl leaned in, lowering her sunglasses.

"Where you headed?" a middle-aged driver asked, smiling at the flash of skin where her coat was still open.

She smiled back: "Where you going?"

He leaned across the seat and opened the door. He watched every inch of her as she climbed in. Focused as he was on her naked flesh, he didn't see her hand dip inside her army bag, where something heavy rested.

There was a flash and a bang from inside the car.

II.

The man's mangled head left a trail of red in the snow as the girl dragged his body well clear of the road.

She was sweating despite her open coat. She let his arms drop, and bent down to dig through his pants, pulling out his wallet—taking out the money, and then studying the address on his ID.

The body lay silent—a ways off, a car engine started, and pulled away.

A modest house.

The yellow car parked in front.

The girl stood under the hot shower, warming up.

She searched through the man's closet, touching all his shirts one by one, finally selecting one.

The sun went down.

Wearing one of his dress shirts now—much too large for her—she checked the fridge. Oranges on a plate. She took a knife from the block and cut one in half on the counter, holding it up and squeezing the sweet juice into her mouth. Then she stood in the center of his living room and, holding her gun in both hands, pressed the barrel against the bony part of her chest between her breasts. She held it like this for quite some time, before tossing it onto the rug.

She curled up on the couch, watching TV.

III.

The Sun rose over the house. The girl came out, once again wearing her long coat and boots. She made sure to lock the door behind her, got in the yellow car and drove off.

Naked wintry trees rolled by outside the windows as she drove the yellow car down the highway, and the cold grey sky reflected in her sunglasses. The engine made a noise, and she looked down. The needle of the gas gauge rested on "E".

The car came to a slow stop by the side of the road, lurching a bit. Then it died. The girl got out, taking her bag, and looked both ways up and down the road.

Far off, the speck of a car appeared, and grew steadily steady larger.

Her fingers began to unbutton her coat.

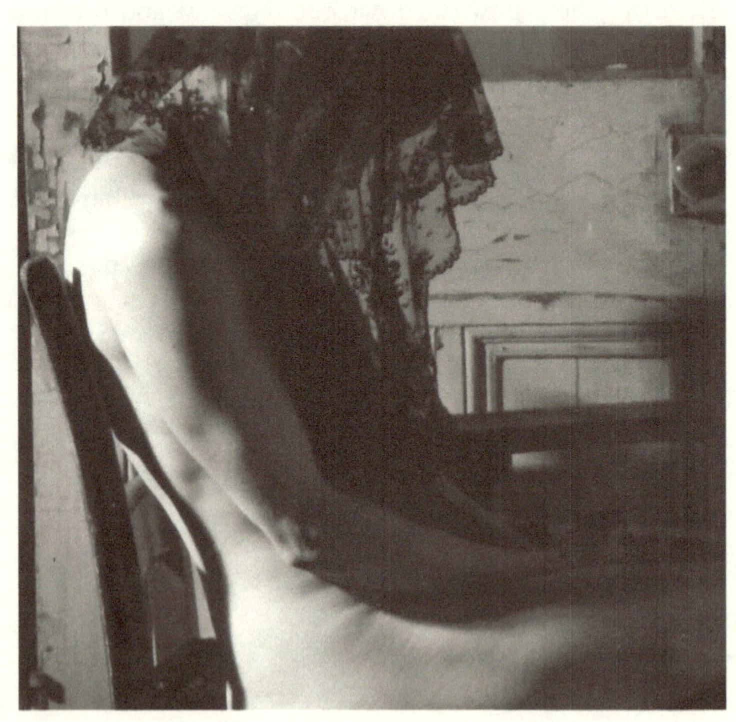

TAKE IT ALL BACK

It was all too late.

Much, much too late.

The damage was done.

The cost was dear.

And now that it was over,

The old man was sorry.

But his sorrow didn't matter.

Because it was all too late.

Much, much too late.

The corpses he'd left behind

Stared at him with blind eyes

And open, questioning mouths.

The damage was done.

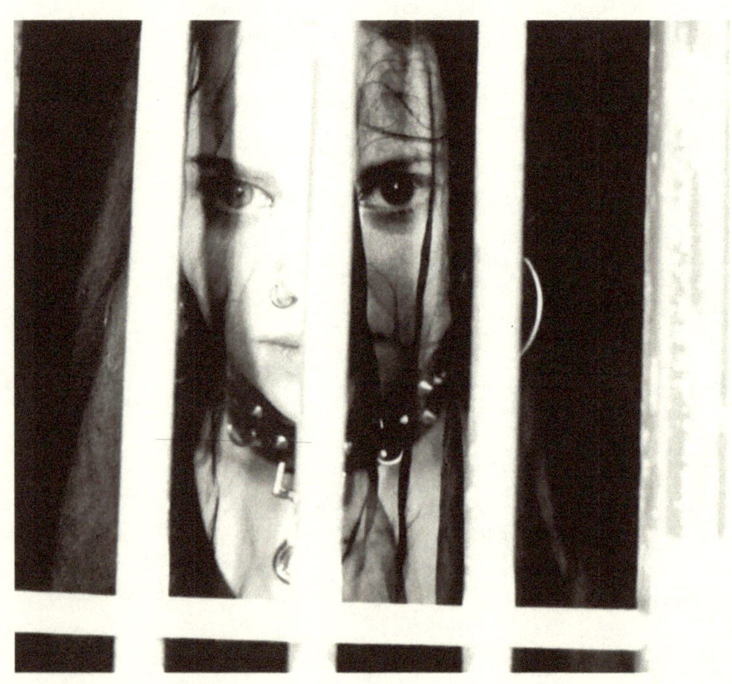

PATHOLOGICAL

He'd met her before, he was sure.

At least twice?

The same bony shoulders,

the same false smile,

the same unfeeling eyes.

Yes, he'd met her before—but with a different name.

From a different place.

Again, the cold look,

hovering hungry as a wraith behind the inviting smile.

A lack of warmth,

of empathy,

lack of just human feeling.

Something he'd always taken for granted natively existed

in other people.

But not this.

This was something else before him entirely.

An alien thing—which had learned to almost perfectly replicate human behavior.

Almost.

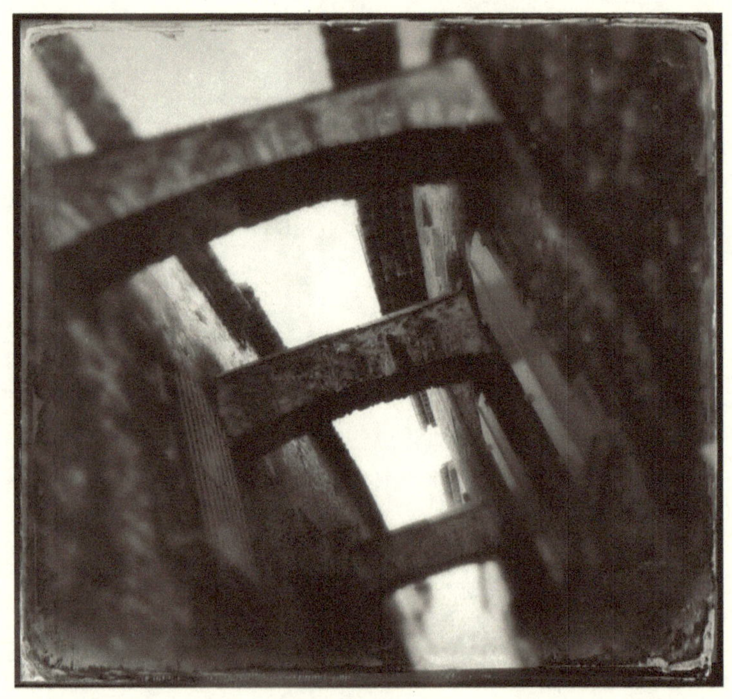

IN A NARROW PLACE

To hell with the excuses and admonitions;

The lies and cajoling, the meaningless blame games

And the mitigating arguments.

Meghan was right the entire time.

We should have listened to her, but we didn't.

Fools.

Damn fools.

To hell with us all.

We held something precious in our fist

And we smashed it on the table, destroying it

Forever.

And now it's gone, and can't be gotten

Back.

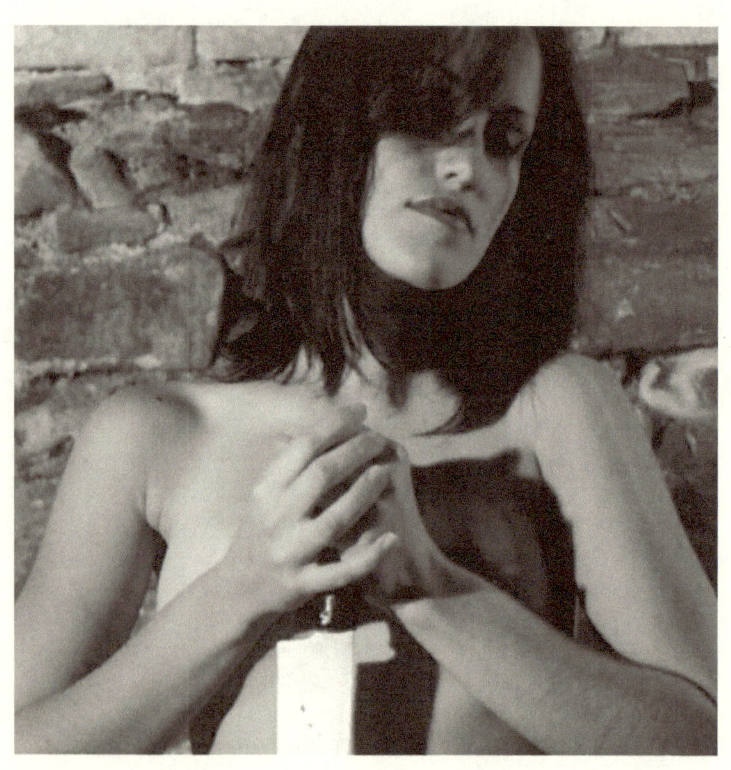

THIS IS NOT THE VOMITORIUM

Her skin burned with fever, but her hands were cold as the dead.

As she carved scrimshaw onto a living man's bones.

(a slow process)

The pain below her rose up in a roar, filling the damp room;

Dark in the corners, glaringly bright in the centre.

But the well of sound was lost on her dead ears;

Long-since deafened by too-long exposure

to all this grotesquerie.

Crimson ichor.

(the scratch of the blade)

Rivulets of sweat pouring down, collecting;

Filling an old paint can on the floor, rusted with years of disuse.

(the lights flickered once)

She kept carving.

WE COULD ALL HAVE DIED A THOUSAND TIMES BY NOW

There are planets where it rains diamonds.

    (razor sharp diamonds)

The astronauts heard music on the far side of the Moon.

Far off and hard to make out;

like looking at your reflection in a tarnished spoon.

The opium smokers have seen things you and I will never understand:

    (they don't either, the poor confused bastards)

Under the right conditions, flour can explode.

The antonym of an antonym is a synonym,

and the grey hairs in my beard continue to grow

    (so many friends who never lived long enough to get them)

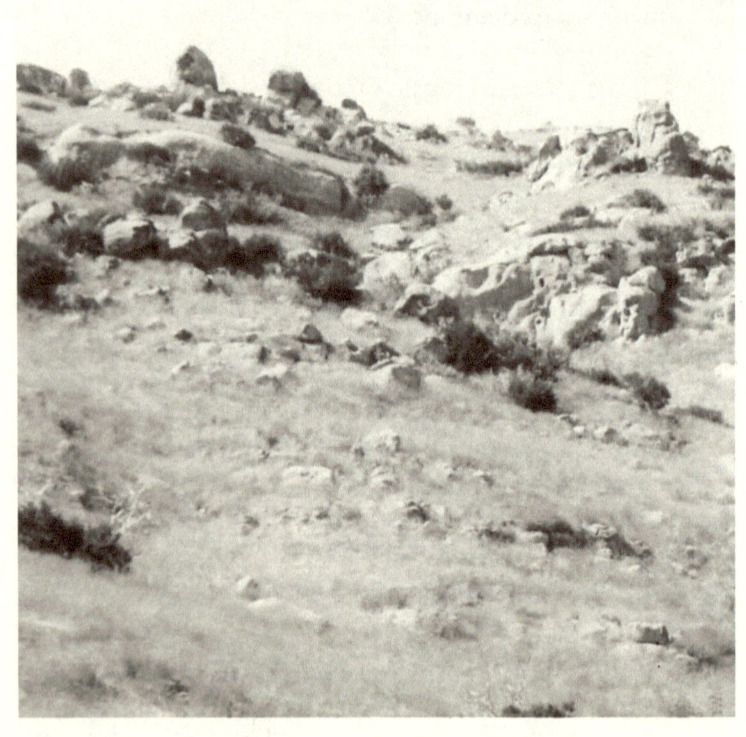

TERMINUS

The jagged cliffs of Vasquez Rocks were a row of lazy needles that leaned against the clear desert sky.

The '75 Chevy Nova Super Sport churned up gravel and dust as it drove up, and then came to a stop. The drivers' door opened and a tall, powerfully built man got out. He wore black slacks with suspenders over a white undershirt, and the white undershirt was spattered with blood. His shaggy black hair blew about in the dry wind. His name was Edison. Looking around a moment, he drew a dull black .45 out of the waistband of his slacks, ejecting the magazine and clearing the chamber before tossing it onto the seat.

He took a few steps away from the car to admire the rock formations, and a second man got out the passenger side. This one was both older and shorter than Edison-an Asian man with a powerful physique and similarly flowing black hair, though his was shot through with grey. This was Stan, and he was the first to speak:

"Pretty impressive, huh? Can't believe you never made it up this way."

Edison turned back:

"I haven't had a lot of time for sightseeing since I came back."

"Sightseeing my ass- this place is great for dumping stiffs. Probably two dozen guys takin' dirt naps under our feet right now."

Edison glanced down at the gritty earth under his weathered boots, and Stan watched the younger man for a long moment.

"You're still thinking about what went down back there. I figured you'd be a lot colder than that by now, after everything..."

Edison shrugged, "It's not that, it's just--" He trailed off, staring around him. Staring at nothing. But old Stan knew what was going on inside.

"You hit the wall, didn't you? That moment where you look down at the shooter in your hand and the whole thing seems one hundred goddamn percent pointless. Pull the trigger, don't pull the trigger. Life, death, no matter."

"Sounds like you've been there."

"Hell... I live there these days, kid."

"So what made you keep doing the job all this time?" Edison asked.

"Well, if you'll remember, I had this little orphan brat to look after. Little bastard needed food, a roof over his head, all kinds of annoying things."

Edison grinned, despite himself: "And he never really appreciated it, did he?"

"He never said as much, no. But I knew he did."

"Right."

Edison's eyes turned once more to the jagged cliffs above. Something was slowly occurring to him. His eyes came back to the hard ground beneath him again- back to the car, and then finally to Old Stan.

"So why did we come all the way out here, Stan?"

Stan smiled a small sad smile. His right hand had casually drifted to the gun tucked in the back of his trousers.

Edison saw it, too. He glanced into the car, where his pistol sat unloaded on the seat, then back at Stan.

"He knows, doesn't he?"

Stan nodded. "Yeah."

"How?"

"How do you think he got to be the in-charge guy? It wasn't by letting the little things get past him."

Even as he spoke, Edison's mind was searching for options.

"Why you?"

"It was gonna happen, son. This way, we figured- well, at least it'll be someone familiar."

"But how can you--?"

"You're a big boy, Ed. You knew what you were messing with, and what the consequences would be. Look at me: I'm way past my prime. What am I gonna do, bag groceries in my twilight years? This is all I know. The Chief made it abundantly clear... when it comes right down to it, I'm the one that brought you into the Circle. I'm responsible. It's you or me, kid, and it's sure as shit ain't gonna be me."

The two men stared at each other. The hot arid breeze kicked up a bit.

"I thought I'd imagined every possible way this scenario could go down..." Edison murmured. "I gotta admit: this wasn't one of them."

Stan shrugged. "None of us ever see it coming. But it comes all the same, in the end. Now do us both a favor and turn around, okay? It'll make it a helluva lot easier, I promise."

Edison turned slowly, raising his hands up, and Stan took a few cautious steps towards him, drawing out his automatic. Edison listened to the sound of his footfalls, waiting. Then he felt the gun muzzle press against the back of his head.

Stan paused a moment before firing. He was fighting back his emotions- willing himself to do what needed doing.

"It's gonna kill me to do this, you know," he finally said.

Edison smiled: "Yeah. I know."

He paused.

"Hey, I want to tell you something... something I've never told you."

Stan's eyebrow raised a quarter inch. "Go on."

The moment hung there, suspended, and then:

"You always wait too long to cock the hammer."

Stan's eyes widened. In half a second, his thumb reached up and cocked the gun, but that was the sound Edison had been waiting for. In a single motion, he spun 'round and grabbed the gun tightly by the slide with his left hand. Stan's finger jerked on the trigger, but the gun wouldn't fire.

Edison snapped the pistol's barrel around one hundred-eighty degrees to point towards Stan, trapping the older man's finger in the trigger guard and breaking it. Stan gave out a wail and immediately sank to his knees.

Edison stared down at his foster father for a moment, his own feelings at war with each other- but only for a moment. He shoved the gun towards Stan several times, pushing the trigger against Stan's broken finger each time.

The gunshots echoed off the jagged cliffs, and Stan's body collapsed to the ground at Edison's feet, the gun hitting the dust a half second after.

Edison struggled to get his body and his emotions back under control, as he stared down at the corpse. It took a full minute and a good deal of effort, but he finally managed to slow his breathing. As he did, he became aware of a barely-audible sound coming from the rear of the Nova. He stepped over the body and went round to the driver's side of the car, taking the keys out of the ignition and moving to the trunk. Opening it, he paused.

Inside was a beautiful young woman, her wrists and ankles tied with zip ties, her mouth taped shut. She'd been crying, and lines of heavy black makeup run down her cheeks like charcoal tears. Her name was Yukari. She was the Chief's wife- and Edison was in love with her.

"Hey, you're not supposed to be here."

He reached into the trunk, and Yukari held out her wrists, assuming he was going to free her, but instead his hand come back holding a shovel.

"Stay put. I'll be right back."

She screamed through the gag and he shut the trunk lid again.

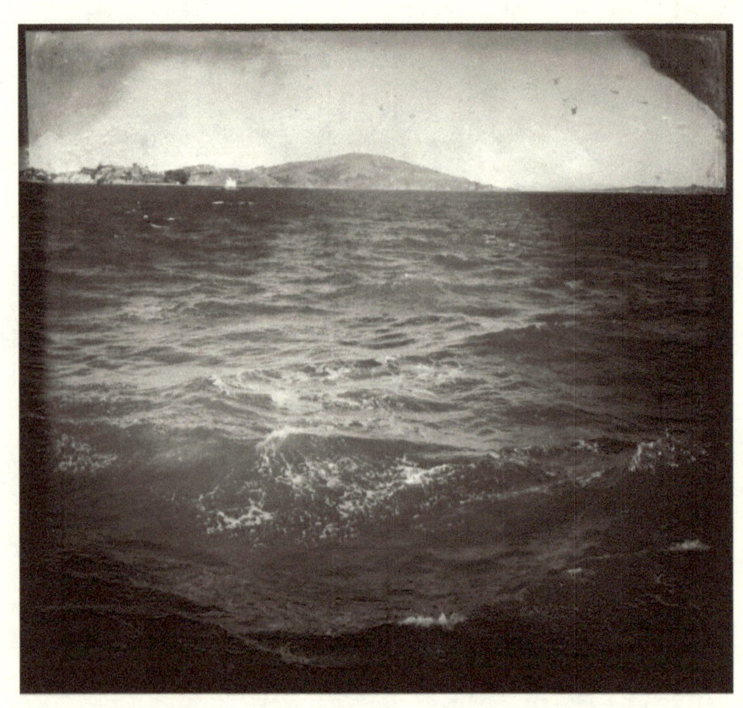

HOLD ON TO YOUR COCKTAILS

Hold onto your cocktails...

This is gonna get hairy.

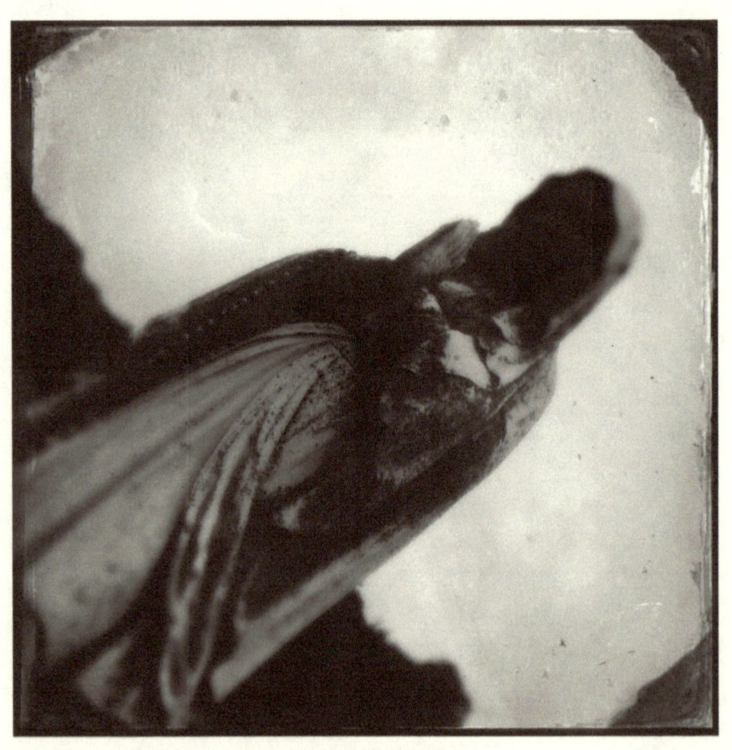

STAN, THE FALLEN

What happened to Stan was a real shame.

He was a pretty nice guy.

Except for all the evil stuff he did, of course.

Has anyone else actually SEEN a hole open up under someone?

Besides in cartoons, of course.

Nice knowing you, Stan.

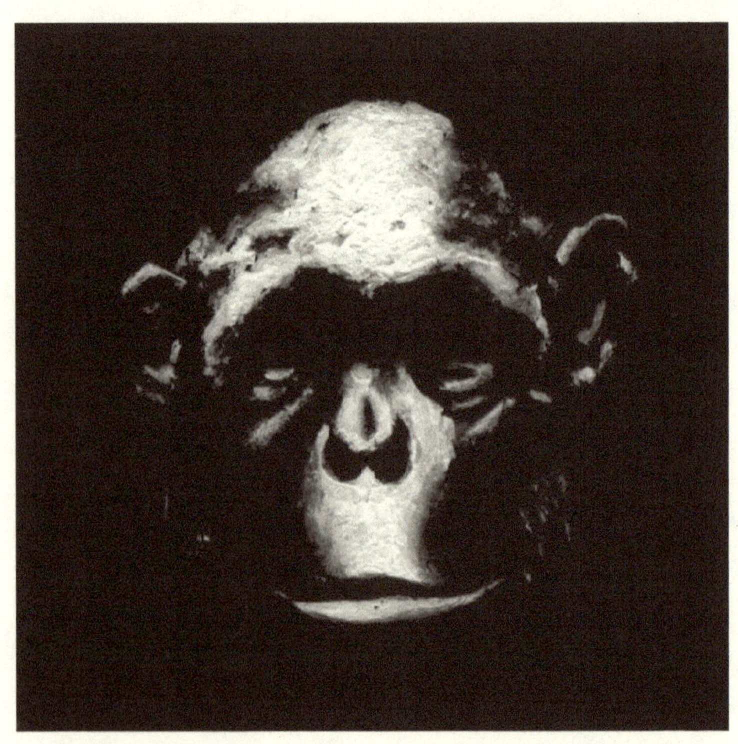

THINGS THE MONKEY KNOWS

The Monkey knows you've been cheating on your diet.

The Monkey knows the nickname that girl made up for you in 5th grade.

The Monkey knows what happened at *The Nutcracker* all those years ago.

The Monkey knows some of your deductions last year were sketchy.

The Monkey knows what you were dreaming about when you woke up at 4 AM.

The Monkey knows what you hid in the basement behind the hot water heater.

The Monkey knows all these things...

...but he still has no idea where he put his keys.

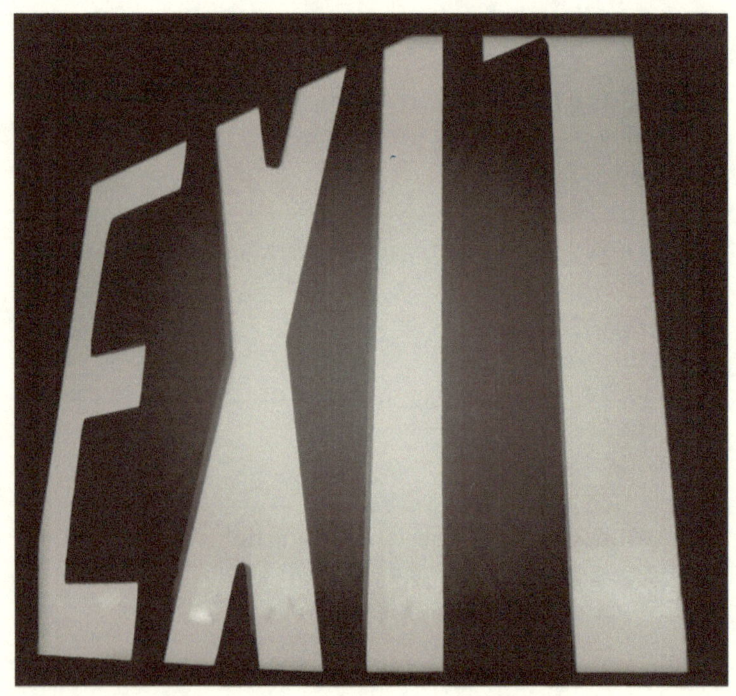
EXIT

OLD FAITHFUL

His head hurt.

A dull throb,

a rhythmic drumbeat.

Somewhere at the base of his skull

it was working its way forward,

like a snake slithering through his brain.

He knew that in the very near future,

it would worm its way through his temples to finally curl

up and rest

behind his eyes.

The pressure would be unbearable.

His own blood would feel like acid.

A hundred thousand tiny razor blades,

slicing their slow way though the nerves of his face.

Each shallow breath would burn more and more,

until there would be no air left;

and unconsciousness would free him from any pain.

And the Next Day,

it would begin

All.

Over.

Again.

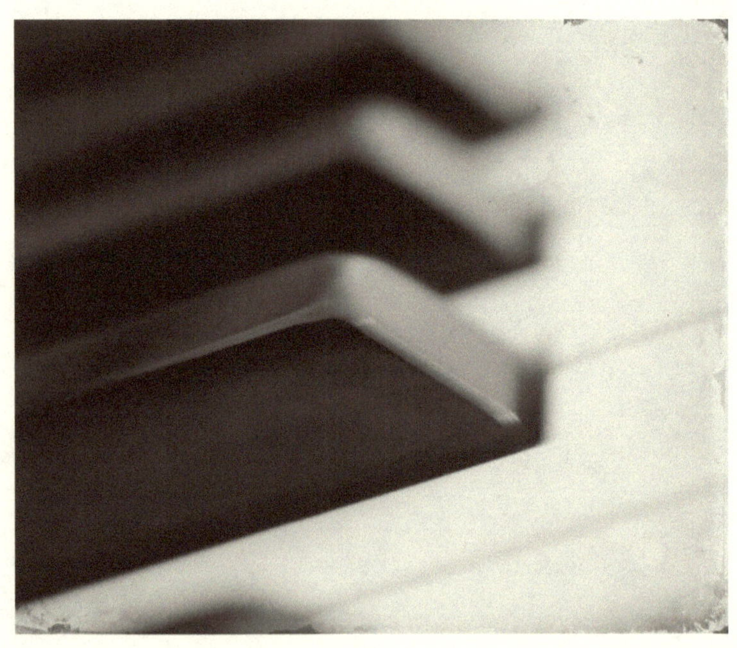

THE PRODIGY

The boy's gifts had been undeniable.

The dance of his fingers on the key of

The old piano

in the drafty front room,

of the run-down house,

had changed everything.

Schools had come calling.

Conservatoires had reached out.

Scholarships.

Invitations to perform.

Then the fire.

Late one night.

No one had escaped.

Everything had burned.

Except, ironically,

The piano.

The burned shell

Of the house

Sat empty for years.

Until someone bought it,

and took the piano home

for their own children to play.

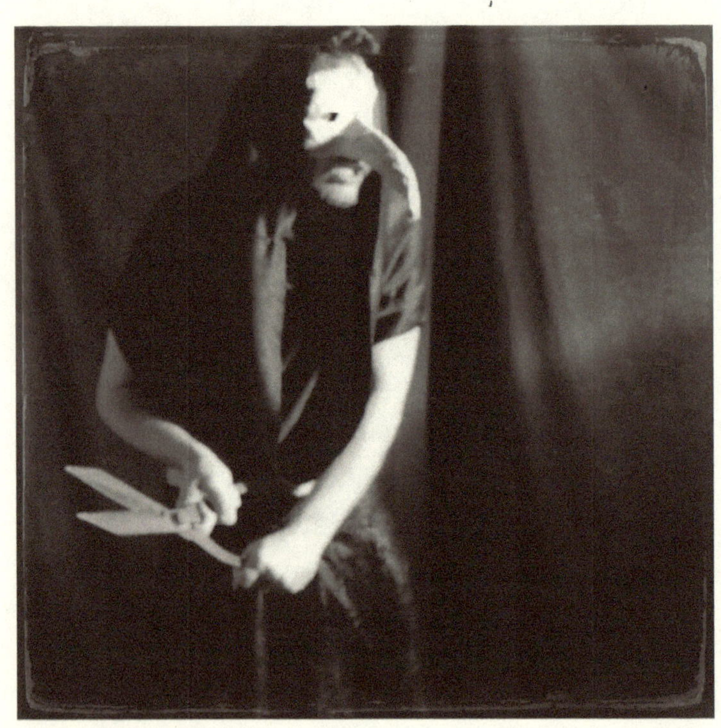

HELL WITH THE LID OFF

She'd disappeared ten years before.

Only five since they'd found her body.

He'd kept her phone. Sometimes, he'd leave her messages.

The police had used up all worldly options,

But could not find her killer.

So he'd turned to the old ways.

He spoke to the seeing sisters,

He'd taken the potions and spent an eternity in the next world,

Only to return to this hell with just a half-hour passed.

He'd made little sacrifices, and carried small totems with him at all times.

The vision had come without warning,

It had been right in front of him all along.

Her killer.

In the guise of a friend.

He'd taken his time:

stalking his friend,

(the way he had done to her).

He was patient, and then the time was right.

He cleansed himself. He made the proper supplications.

The knife was intentionally dull.

But all the blood in the world didn't make it better.

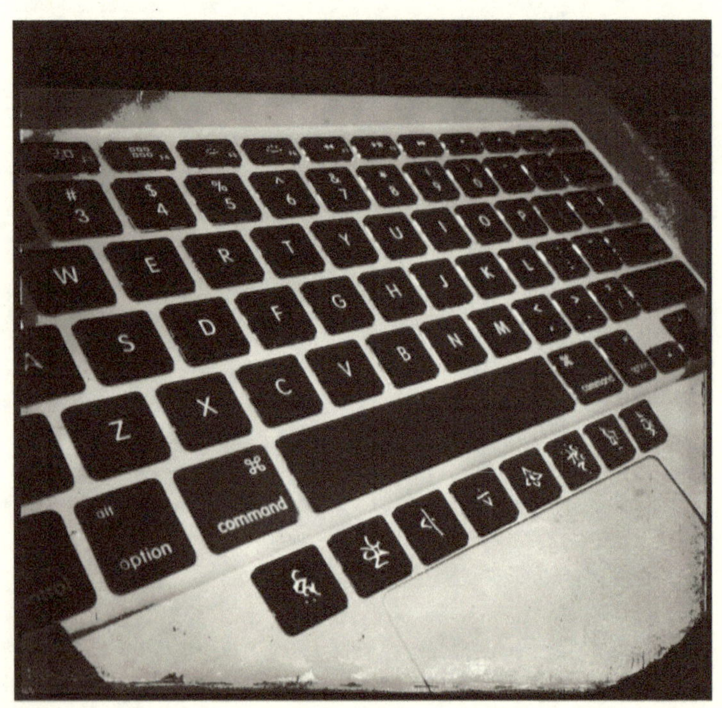

W E R T Y U I O P
S D F G H J K L
Z X C V B N M
alt
option
command

SECRET KEYS

I had a dream last night

That I discovered an entirely new row of keys on my laptop,

Labeled with strange characters,

With which I could spell new and unknown things.

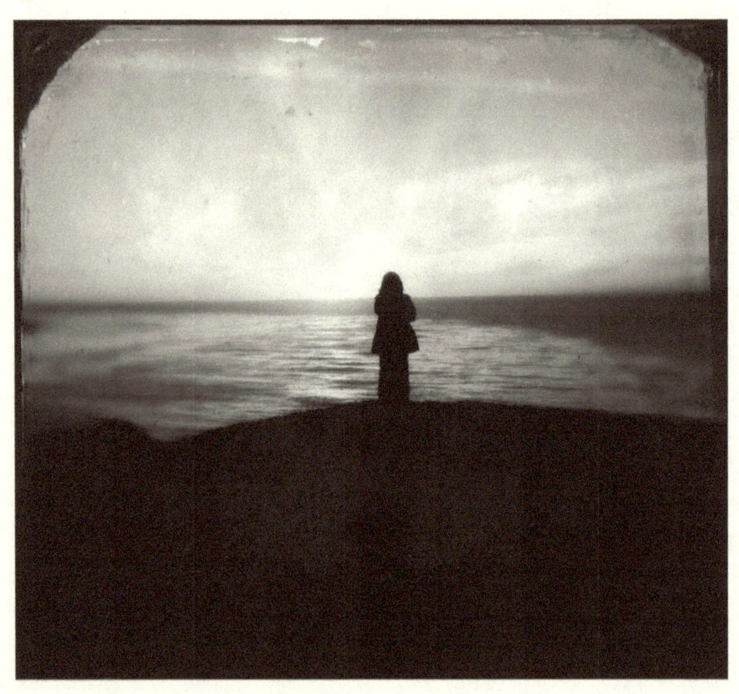

ONE OF THE LIVING

She raises me up out of this.

She takes away the woe of years:

the strain, the privation, the doubt.

Even for just a few moments.

Which is more than enough.

Like a time-traveller out of the past,

or maybe the future.

A Technicolor girl,

In my black and white world.

About the Author

Jim Towns is a writer, director and artist. His films include the silent expressionist feature *Prometheus Triumphant: a Fugue in the Key of Flesh*, the necromantic dark comedy *STIFF*, the award-winning haunted heist film *House of Bad*, the post-apocalyptic drama *State of Desolation*, and the streaming series *Immortal Hands*.

His published short fiction includes "Warlock's Eye" (FunDead Publications), "Fools at the Feet of a Hanged Man" (*Dodging the Rain* literary magazine), "Castrato" (*Things in the Well),* "The Grave" (Hellbound Books) and "Bad Coffee and the Bomb" (*Switchblade Magazine*). 2020 saw the publication of his debut nonfiction book, *American Cryptic.*

His paintings and mixed media artwork have been exhibited in galleries in Pittsburgh, New York and Los Angeles.

He currently lives in San Pedro, CA with his wife and two mysterious cats.

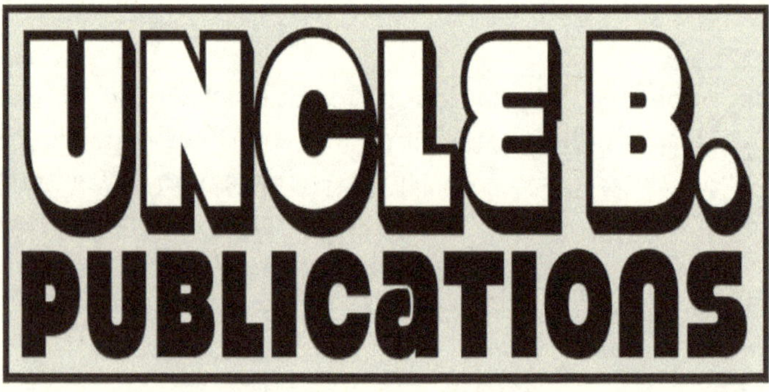

An Indianapolis-based
Publishing Mafia

www.ingramcontent.com/pod-product-compliance
Lightning Source LLC
LaVergne TN
LVHW051014080826
845145LV00009B/2608

* 9 7 8 1 9 5 7 0 3 4 0 5 8 *